Written by Judy Oetting • Illustrated by Larry Nolte

Cover design by Gray Communications

Printed in the United States of America by Comfort Printing
10 9 8 7 6 5 4 3 2 1

Meet Digger

Digger is a mole. Moles are small, furry mammals that live underground most of the time. They eat insects and worms. Their very small eyes cannot see well, but their short front legs have strong digging claws that can dig a tunnel through your yard in a hurry.

Digger is going to introduce you to rock collecting and help you discover the rocks, minerals, and fossils of Missouri. Count by 2's to draw Digger.

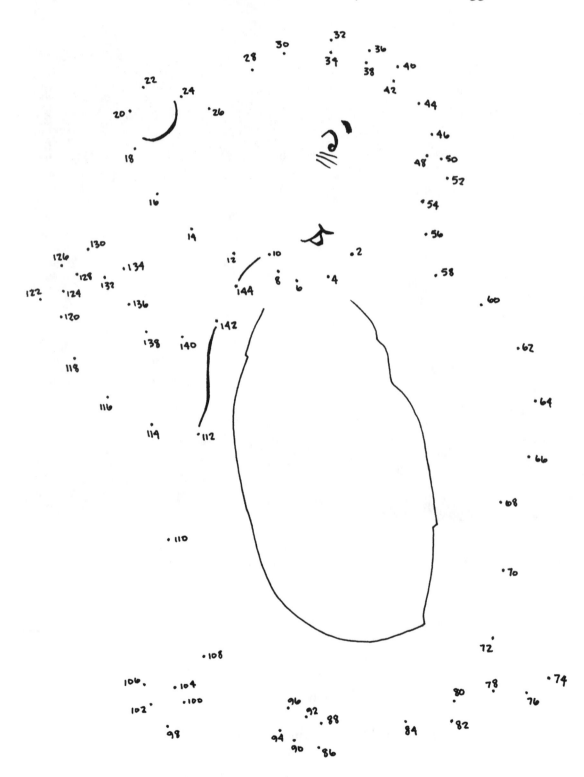

It's Batty

Batty B. Bat can catch 600 mosquitoes in an hour. Bats that are like Batty can live to be 30 years old. Most bats produce only one baby a year. This makes it easy for bats to become extinct. Many people are afraid of bats because they think they will fly into their hair, but they won't. Bats send out signals that bounce back to them. This shows them where things are, so they never run into things. Batty is going to help you explore some features of caves.

Batty likes the number 3. Count by 3's to draw Batty. Draw a line between 168 and 0 to finish.

Ain't Nothin' but a Rock Hound

Digger is a "rock hound." A rock hound is someone who collects rocks.

Design a T-shirt for Digger that shows he's one of Missouri's best rock hounds.

"I Dig Rocks"

"Sweeter Than Rock Candy"

"I'm Off My Rocker"

"Rock Fever"

"Rock Around The Clock"

"Rocking Rascal"

"Watch Out For Falling Rocks"   "Rock and Roll"   "Rock Bottom"

"Where Did My Words Go?"

Digger left his tool list in the rain.

Fill in the missing parts of the letters
to find out what he needs.

NEWSPAPER
HAND LENS
BAG
HAMMER
CHISEL
SAFETY GOGGLES
HEAVY GLOVES
GUIDE BOOK
CHOCOLATE BAR

HEY, DIGGER!
WHAT KIND OF TOOL
IS CHOCOLATE?

IT IS MY
TUMMY TOOL!

I DIDN'T KNOW
MOLES ATE
CHOCOLATE?

WE DON'T! I USE
CHOCOLATE TO ATTRACT
ANTS. I LIKE ANTS!

Tool Time

Someone hid Digger's tools.

Read about Digger's rock collecting tools.
Then circle them in the picture below.

You should find nine objects.

Safety goggles — to keep rock chips out of people's eyes.
Heavy gloves — to keep from getting cuts and scrapes.
Hand lens — to closely see the small rocks, minerals, and fossils.
Field guide — to identify rock or mineral specimens.
Hammer — to extract (pull out) the rock or mineral specimen.
Chisels — to cut through solid rock. *(There are two chisels in the picture below.)*
Newspaper — to wrap up specimens and keep them safe.
Bag — to carry the specimens. *(This can be a carrying bag or a paper bag.)*

"What should I wear?"

Digger needs help picking the right clothes to wear for rock hunting.

Circle the correct accessory or outfit in each set.

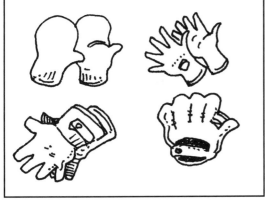

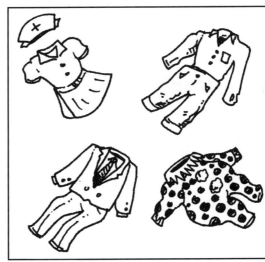

DO I LOOK READY FOR ROCK HUNTING?

NO, YOU LOOK READY FOR THE CIRCUS!

Shadow Tools

Moles don't see well in sunshine.
Digger has to look at shadows.

Draw a line from the real object to its shadow so Digger can find the right tools.

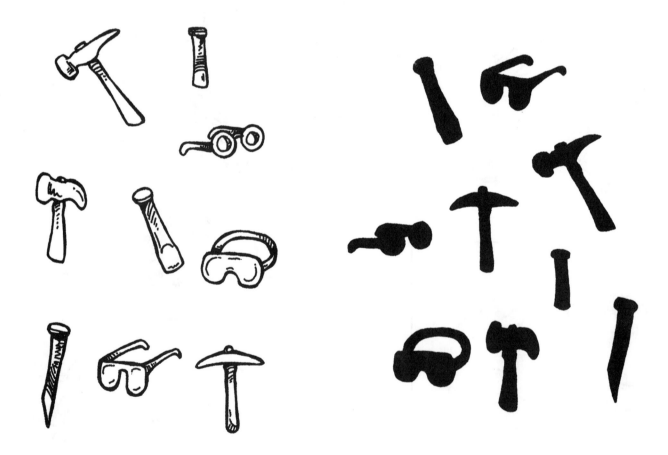

An A"maze"ing Journey!

Help Digger find gold.

Guide him on a journey through Missouri's Platte River to the gold nuggets.

"Wow! I'm Getting Brighter Every Day!"

Identify the three major types of rocks on the following page.
Find the right letter for each picture.

A

C

D

E

G

H

I

M

N

O

P

R

S

T

U

Y

___ ___ ___ ___ ___ ___ ___ ___ ___ ___ ___ ___

___ ___ ___ ___ ___ ___ ___ ___ ___ ___ ___

___ ___ ___ ___ ___ ___ ___

Digger *Digs* Rocks

Help Digger find ten of Missouri's rocks and minerals.
Look for the words across, down, and diagonally.

R F L U O R I T E M A

D I M B S U V P O N I

G N C A L C I T E H U

L M H N V K S L P O S

P X U K A L A H A C I

Y P M V A G A T E S L

R H G Y C L E J X C V

I W V O I D N O Y H E

T X A Y L C F R D S R

E N U W I D S N L E M

Q U A R T Z B V G O I

V A M E T H Y S T P B

Word List

Agate

Amethyst

Calcite

Fluorite

Galena

Geode

Gold

Pyrite

Quartz

Silver

Everything's Backward!

Ten of Missouri's rocks are spelled backward.

Draw a line from the backward rock to the "rite" rock. The first one has been done for you.

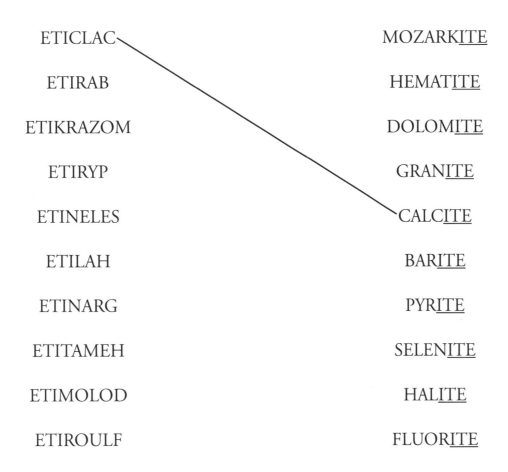

ETICLAC	MOZARK<u>ITE</u>
ETIRAB	HEMAT<u>ITE</u>
ETIKRAZOM	DOLOM<u>ITE</u>
ETIRYP	GRAN<u>ITE</u>
ETINELES	CAL<u>CITE</u>
ETILAH	BAR<u>ITE</u>
ETINARG	PYR<u>ITE</u>
ETITAMEH	SELEN<u>ITE</u>
ETIMOLOD	HAL<u>ITE</u>
ETIROULF	FLUOR<u>ITE</u>

Mood Rocks

Draw a face on each rock to match the mood word.

Example:

Happy

Sad

Mad

Mean

Surprised

Scared

Funny

Angelic

Draw the look your mom or dad would have on his or her face if you got dirty digging for rocks.

Making things a little brighter

Find the crystal treasure for Digger.
Follow the directions below.

1. Draw a line from 1 to 2.
2. Draw a line from 1 to 3.
3. Draw a line from 1 to 5.
4. Draw a line from 1 to 6.
5. Draw a line from 5 to 2.
6. Draw a line from 2 to 3.
7. Draw a line from 3 to 6.
8. Draw a line from 2 to 4.
9. Draw a line from 3 to 4.
10. Draw a line from 5 to 4.
11. Draw a line from 6 to 4.

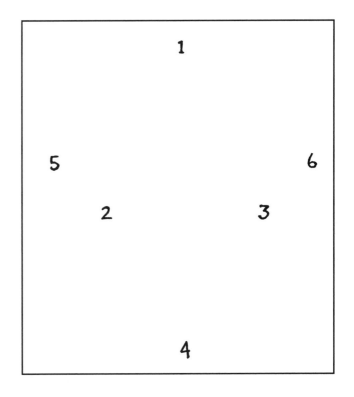

SPARKLE, SPARKLE
LITTLE ROCK.
BRIGHTEN UP MY
TUNNEL DARK!

"What do I need?"

Circle the eight items Digger needs when he goes rock collecting.

What does this say?

Unscramble the names of eight rock collecting tools for Digger.

avhye voelgs

dnah elsn

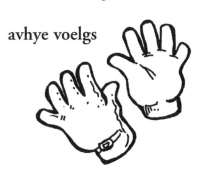

mahmer

_ _ _ _ _ _ _ _ _

_ _ _ _ _ _
_ _ _ _ _ _

_ _ _ _ _ _

gab

feasty sgelgog

hiscel

_ _ _

_ _ _ _ _ _

_ _ _ _ _ _

panwesper

digeu

_ _ _ _ _ _ _ _ _

_ _ _ _ _

What's So Heavy?

Missouri is one of the world's largest producers of

_____.

Find the answer by coloring all the shapes that have a number 1 in them.

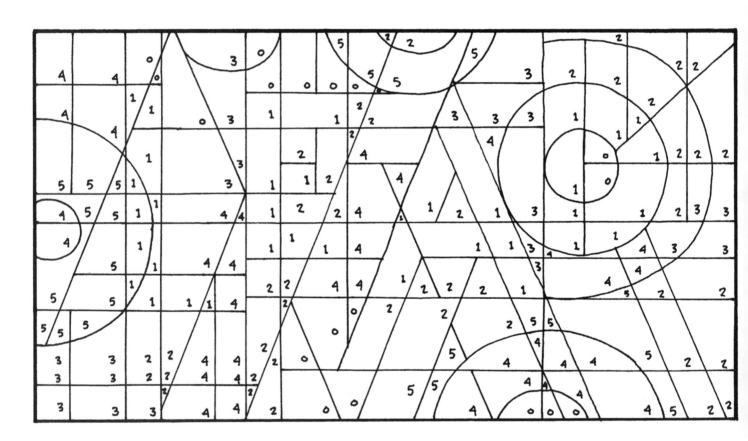

SO, THAT'S WHY THIS BAG WOULDN'T BUDGE!

18

IT'S HUGE!

What is Missouri's biggest fossil?

Match the picture with the correct letter to find out.

A D M N O S T

IT'S A 100 TIMES BIGGER THAN ME!

__ __ __ __ __ __ __ __ __

19

Can you find the fossils?

Find these Missouri fossils in the puzzle below:

BLASTOID, BRACHIOPOD, BRYOZOAN,
CEPHALOPOD, CRINOID, GASTROPOD,
MASTODON, PECCARY, PELECYPOD,
SLOTH, TRILOBITE

They can be found across and down.

O	T	U	F	R	J	L	C	B	S	K	N	B	A	P
I	W	T	R	I	L	O	B	I	T	E	G	R	H	E
B	R	A	C	H	I	O	P	O	D	A	D	Y	V	L
D	C	N	T	J	K	L	N	I	M	J	M	O	L	E
M	A	S	T	O	D	O	N	Y	I	C	W	Z	S	C
Y	W	R	P	G	O	I	W	C	J	D	Z	O	L	Y
P	E	C	C	A	R	Y	R	H	L	I	M	A	F	P
W	J	O	V	H	J	O	Q	B	K	J	X	N	P	O
R	M	L	C	R	I	N	O	I	D	M	R	L	A	D
L	O	W	M	I	O	J	K	F	U	S	L	O	T	H
H	B	L	A	S	T	O	I	D	L	A	L	U	S	E
B	K	M	S	H	G	A	S	T	R	O	P	O	D	F
C	E	P	H	A	L	O	P	O	D	S	U	E	I	H

"What's my name?"

Use Digger's code to find the names of some common Missouri fossils.

SECRET CODE: A⠄ B⠆ C⠒ D⠢ E⠂ G⠶ H⠒ I⠲ L⠄⠄ N⠈ O⠶ P⠗

R⠿ S⠦ T⠿

HEY! WHO PUT MY NAME
ON THIS LIST? I'M NOT
A FOSSIL YET!

WHAT DO THESE FOSSILS LOOK LIKE?

Read the sentences below for clues.
Then write the name of each fossil under its picture.

1. A *trilobite* is a strange looking bug.

2. A *crinoid stem* often looks like a stack of little checkers.

3. A *gastropod* has a snail-like shell.

4. This *plant fossil* has leaves.

5. A *brachiopod* looks like it has wings.

6. The end of a *blastoid* looks like a flower.

_____   _____   _____

_____   _____   _____

Can you find the hidden words?

Find the little words hidden inside the names of these Missouri rocks, minerals, or fossils. Circle only those words with two or more letters. The first one has been done for you.

Agate

Anthracite

Amethyst

Quartz

Echinoidea

Elephant Rocks

Magnetite

Pumice

Fool's Gold

Flint

Galena

Gypsum

Granite

Graphite

Halite

Hornblende

Limestone

Trilobite

Crinoid

Mozarkite

Olivine

"DOES IT BITE?"

Color the boxes as follows and find out what has made Digger so afraid.

B=Black
Y=Yellow
L=Blue

```
L L L L L L L L L Y Y Y L L L L L L L L L
L L L L L B L Y Y Y Y Y Y Y L B L L L L L L
L L L L B B B Y Y B Y B Y Y B B B L L L L
L L L B B B B B Y B B B Y B B B B B L L L
L L B B B B B B B B B B B B B B B B B L L
L L B B B B B B B B B B B B B B B B B L L
L B B B Y B B B B B B B B B B Y B B B L
L B B L Y Y B Y B B B B B Y B Y Y L B B L
L B B L L Y Y Y Y B B B Y Y Y Y L L L B L
L L L L L Y Y Y Y Y B Y Y Y Y Y L L L L L
L L L L L L L L Y Y Y Y Y Y Y Y L L L L L L
L L L L L L L L Y Y Y Y Y Y Y L L L L L L L
L L L L L L L L L L Y Y Y L L L L L L L L L
```

COMING OUT OF THE DARK

Batty B. Bat can't see in the dark. Batty sends out sounds that bounce back if something is in his path. This sonar keeps Batty from running into things.

Can you help Batty find his way out of the cave?

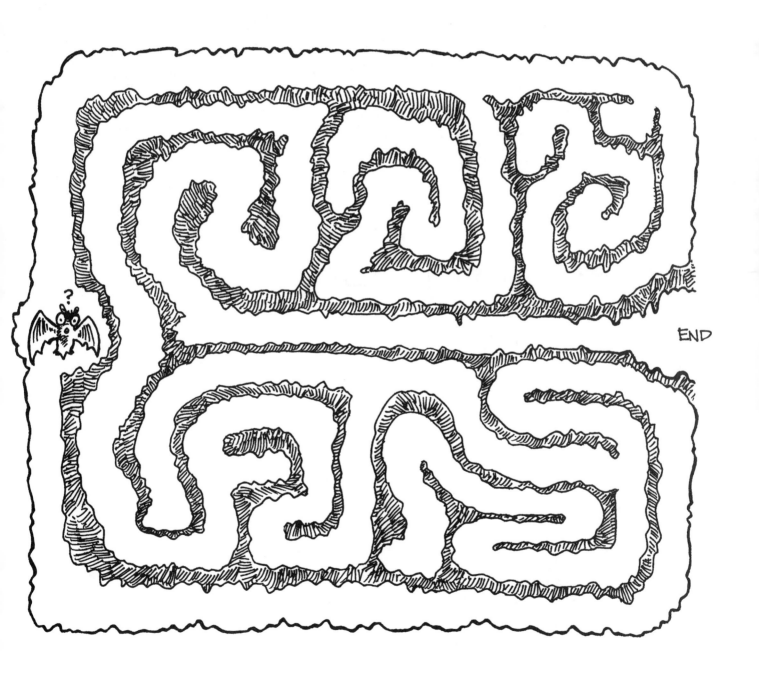

END

Batty's Three Dot Code

Use Batty's three dot code to find the names of some of Batty's Missouri friends.
Write the letter that goes with each symbol in the correct blank.

Code:

⋯	∶ᐧ	⋮	ᐟᐧ
A	E	I	O

THREE, THREE, THREE IS MY LUCKY NUMBER!

OZ☐RK   B☐G-☐ ☐R☐D   B☐T

GR☐Y   B☐T

E☐ST☐RN   P☐P☐STR☐LL   B☐T

☐ND☐ ☐N☐   B☐T

B ☐ G   BR☐WN   B☐T

26

Missouri's nickname

Missouri is called the Show-Me State, but it has another name. It is also called the _____ State. Find the answer by coloring all the shapes that have the letter C in them.

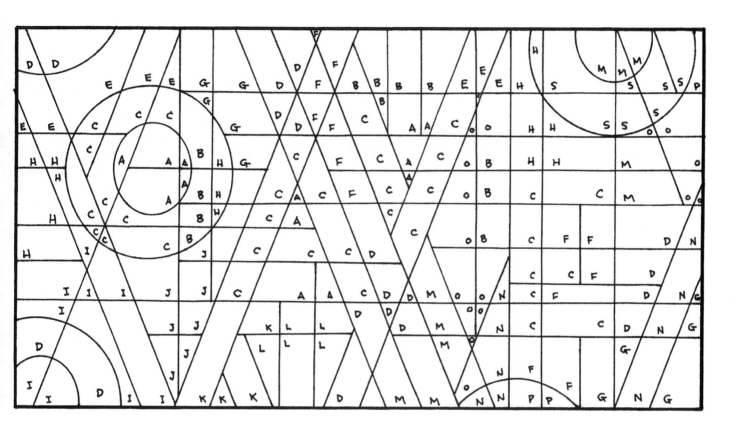

At last count, Missouri had more than 7,200 caves.

"I wonder what these are called?"

Read the descriptions for the cave formations.
Write the number beside the correct formation in the boxes below.

1. A <u>stalactite</u> is a formation that grows from the ceiling.

2. A <u>stalagmite</u> is a formation that grows from the floor of the cave.

3. A <u>column</u> forms when a stalactite meets a stalagmite.

4. <u>Soda straws</u> look like thick straws hanging from cave ceilings with water droplets on the end.

5. A <u>rimstone dam</u> may have a pool of water inside.

6. <u>Cave pearls</u> are round and form inside rimstone dams.

7. Stone <u>lily pads</u> also form in rimstone dams.

8. <u>Helictites</u> have strange shapes and designs like coral.

9. Cave <u>popcorn</u> formations are also called grapes or cauliflower.

10. <u>Drapery</u> formations almost look like real drapes.

Fun Facts

Fill in the blanks in these sentences with one of the following words for cave formations:

Rimstone Dams, Lily Pads, Stalactites, Stalagmites, Helictites, Columns, Draperies, Cave Pearls, Soda Straws, Popcorn.

Look for "Batty" hints in quotation marks.

WATCH OUT! FORMATIONS AHEAD!

1. _____ hold "**tight**" to the cave ceiling.

2. _____ "**might**" make it to the cave ceiling.

3. When stalactites meet stalagmites, you "**call em**" _____ .

4. You won't want to "**drape**" these _____ in your bedroom window.

5. We don't think "**cave**" women wore these _____ around their necks.

6. These _____ would look like miniatures beside the big "**dam**" at Truman Lake.

7. These formations look like _____ on cave walls, but you can't "**pop**" them in your mouth.

8. These are beautifully tangled formations, but don't "**lick**" them. They are very fragile and called _____ .

9. Simple types of hollow stalactites look like _____ , but don't use them to "**sip a soda.**"

10. Cave salamanders might rest on _____ , but these kind of "**pads**" are made of stone.

"What kind of spineless creature are you?"

I AM NOT SPINE, SPINE, SPINELESS! I HAVE A BACK, BACK, BACKBONE!

Draw a line from the name of the creature without a spine (backbone) to the matching sentence.

CAVE SPIDER

A centipede has one pair of legs on each segment. This creature has two pairs of legs on each segment.

CAVE CRAYFISH

Don't let this noisy creature keep you awake.

CAVE MILLIPEDE

It's an eight-legged arachnid.

GROUND BEETLE

This nighttime insect likes the dark.

HERALD MOTH

Pick this creature up carefully. It has pinchers.

CAVE CRICKET

This creature has a "bee" in its name.

"Spineless Creatures Live in My Cave."

CAN YOU FIND, FIND, FIND ONE CREATURE WITH A SPINE, SPINE, SPINE?

Find and circle the cave creatures hidden in the puzzle.

They can be found across, down, and diagonally.

WORD LIST

Bat
Crayfish
Cricket
Millipede
Moth
Salamander
Spider

```
B  H  S  N  C  A  M  T  J  K
L  V  A  P  R  V  H  P  I  X
M  I  L  L  I  P  E  D  E  B
O  L  A  V  C  D  I  T  N  D
T  A  M  I  K  R  E  L  Y  P
H  G  A  K  E  S  F  R  F  Q
Y  V  N  L  T  D  H  B  V  J
X  H  D  G  I  M  R  B  A  T
G  O  E  M  J  K  D  M  P  O
U  C  R  A  Y  F  I  S  H  D
```

I, I, I HAVE A SPINE, SPINE, SPINE.

What can be found in a cave?

I KNOW, KNOW, KNOW!
ASK ME, ME, ME!!

Write a list of things found in a cave.
Give yourself five points for each correct answer.

_____   _____

_____   _____

_____   _____

_____   _____

_____   _____

WHAT'S YOUR SCORE?
WANT TO TRY FOR
MORE?

BATTY'S CAVE

Circle the five differences in the pictures below.

BUILD WITH WORDS

See how many words you can make from STALACTITE and then from STALAGMITE.
Write them in the columns below. Put the words they have in common in the center column.

STALACTITE

late
___

cat
___

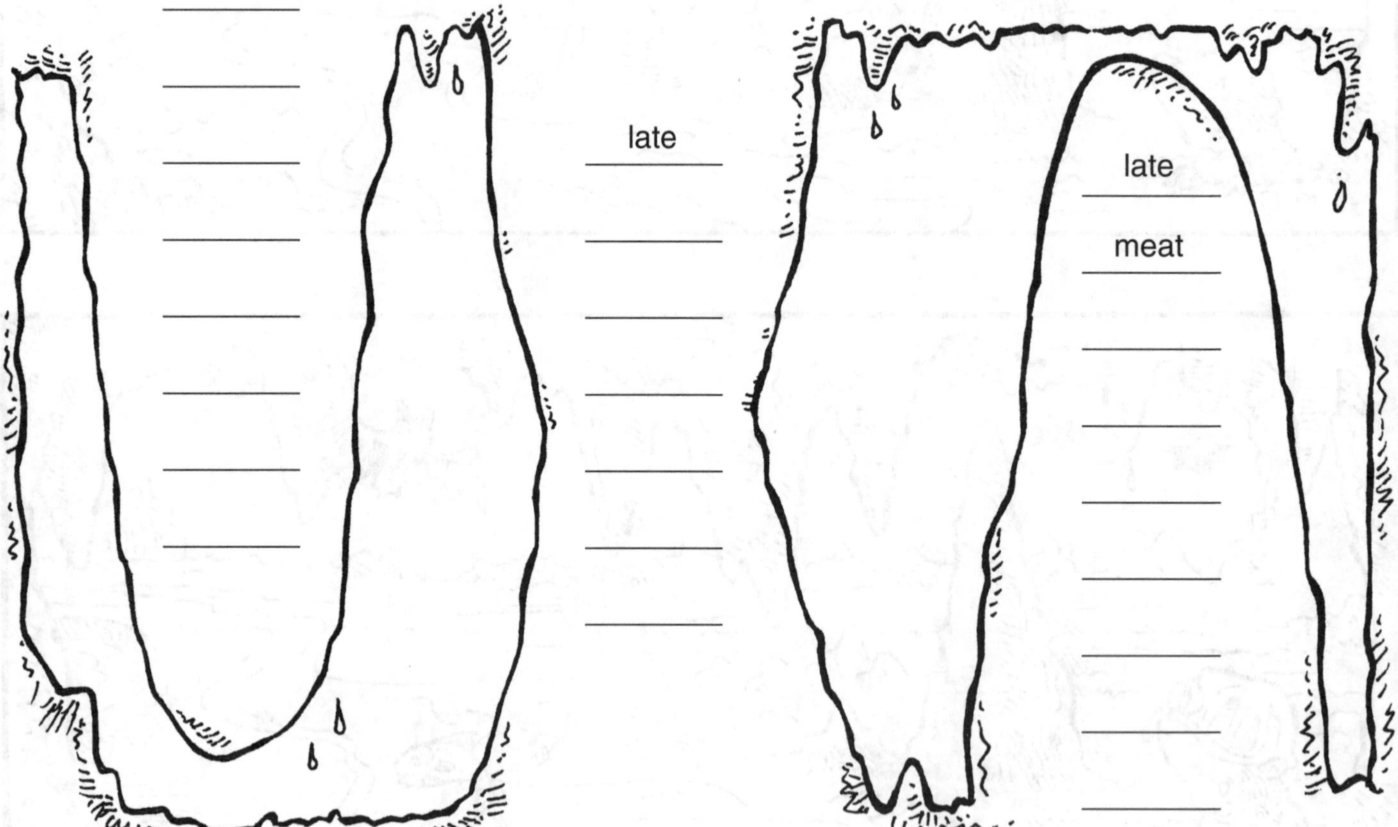

___

___

___

___

___

___

___

late
___

___

___

___

___

late
___

meat
___

___

___

___

___

___

___

___

STALAGMITE

Watch out!
It's an earthquake!

Seismologists are scientists who study faults and earthquakes. They use instruments called seismographs to record the motion of the ground and measure the magnitude of an earthquake. Seismologists use the Richter scale to describe the earthquake's magnitude. Earthquakes are measured on a scale from 1 to 10.

Missouri had a big earthquake in 1811. It measured _____ on the Richter scale.

Find the answer by coloring all the shapes that have the letter "C" in them BLUE.

"I want to be a ____gist when I grow up!"

Each word below is the name of a special kind of scientist.

Count the letters in each name and match them to a definition.

GET THE GIST?

WORD LIST
ARCHAEOLOGIST, GEOLOGIST, PALEONTOLOGIST, METALLURGIST,
METEOROLOGIST, SEISMOLOGIST, SPELEOLOGIST

1. A scientist that studies fossil plants and animals.
__ __ __ __ __ __ __ __ __ G I S T

2. A scientist that studies rocks, gems, and minerals.
__ __ __ __ G I S T

3. A scientist that studies the art of working with metals.
__ __ T __ __ __ __ __ G I S T

4. A scientist that studies caves.
__ __ __ __ __ __ __ __ G I S T

5. A scientist that studies earthquakes.
__ __ __ S __ __ __ __ G I S T

6. A scientist that studies ancient artifacts like pottery and spear points.
__ __ C __ __ __ __ __ __ __ G I S T

7. A scientist that studies the weather.
__ __ __ __ __ __ __ __ __ G I S T

All Cracked Up

Help! An earthquake just cracked these words in half.

Can you connect the word parts with a line
before Batty B. Bat falls off the stalactite?
The first word part has been connected for you.

YIKES!!

SEDI	MORPHIC
MINE	CK
EARTH	QUAKE
RO	SIL
FOS	RAL
META	OUS
IGNE	MENTARY

The Earth Is Moving!

Make as many words as you can from the letters in the word
EARTHQUAKES. Make words with three or more letters in them.
Put the words in the right column.

three-letter words	four-letter words	five-letter words
art	heat	quake
_____	_____	_____
_____	_____	_____
_____	_____	_____
_____	_____	_____
_____	_____	_____
_____	_____	_____
_____	_____	_____
_____	_____	_____

I THOUGHT ALL THE EARTHQUAKES WERE IN CALIFORNIA.

NO, DIGGER, MISSOURI HAS A FAULT CALLED NEW MADRID WHERE EARTHQUAKES HAVE OCCURRED.

WELL, IT'S NOT MY FAULT!

SINCE YOU LIVE IN MISSOURI, DIGGER, IT'S YOUR FAULT, TOO!

THAT'S NOT FAIR!

"I dig, you dig, we all dig rocks."

You can do this alone, but it is more fun with friends.
Find as many things on this list as you can.

Then get a book on rocks and minerals and try to identify them.
Label them and your collection has begun.

1. Find a rock smaller than your thumbnail. The sand pile is a great place to look.

2. Look for a rock larger than your fist.

3. Find a rock with shiny quartz crystals. Check out the rocks in your driveway.

4. Dig a hole in a rocky area and find a rock with different colors or layers.

5. Find the softest rock you can. If you can scratch it with your fingernail or a coin, it is considered to be a soft rock.

6. Find the hardest rock you can. If you can't scratch it with a steel pocket knife, it is considered to be a hard rock. Get your parents' permission before you use a knife.

7. Look for a rock that has fossils. Check out the rocks used as decorations in yards or in the driveway.

8. Look for a rock with holes or strange shapes. Get your parents and take a walk beside a streambed.

2 + 1 = ?

Help Digger solve these math problems.
Put the answer in the space provided.

1. Digger took *1 hand lens, 1 guide book,* and *2 hammers* on his trip.
   How many rock collecting tools did he take? _____

2. Digger had a bag filled with *10 pieces of quartz.* On his way home, he dropped *2 pieces.* How many pieces did Digger have left? _____

3. Digger discovered some fossils in a creek near his home. He found *1 blastoid, 2 trilobites, 1 crinoid,* and *3 plant fossils.* How many fossils did he find all together?
   _____

4. Digger's friend Batty brought him *1 geode, 1 piece of gold,* and *3 pieces of pyrite.* How many rocks and minerals did Batty bring him? _____

5. Batty flew into his cave and noticed these formations: *2 stalactites, 3 stalagmites, 1 column,* and *1 drapery.* How many formations were in his cave? _____

We Can Learn
from the Rocks in the Earth

Read the paragraph below and find where the underlined words fit in the puzzle.
All the words will read across.

The earth is a giant storybook. We turn the <u>layers</u> of the earth to find out about the <u>rocks</u> and <u>minerals</u> beneath our feet. Many are <u>beautiful</u> and valuable. We use mineral <u>ores</u> daily in homes, cars, industry, and science. They are one of our important <u>natural</u> <u>resources</u>.

Rocks and Minerals Are Useful

Follow the directions to cross out words in the following lists.
The words that are left are things that are made with rocks or minerals.

1. Cross out the names of flowers.

2. Cross out the names of creatures with legs.

3. Cross out anything you can warm up to drink.

4. Cross out a word beginning with "W."

Jewelry	Rose	Centipede	Salt
Worm	Sheet Rock	Tulip	Pans
Paper	Plumbing Pipes	Money	Millipede
Violet	China Dishes	Tea	Bricks
Cement	Dandelion	Soap	Trumpet
Batteries	Beetles	Sunscreen	Cans
Foil	Coffee	Paint	Medicine

"Want to Borrow My Thinking Cap?"

Search these sentences for names associated with Missouri rocks and minerals and circle them.

Part of a name may be found at the end of one word with the rest of the name at the beginning of the next word. The first sentence has been done for you.

<u>Word List</u>
Agate, ~~Chert,~~ Galena, Gold, Lead, Mineral, Talc

1. The teacher tried to talk to my mom, but she was gone.

2. Dale admits he is afraid to sing a solo.

3. The big antlered stag ate moss from the rocky soil.

4. During the windy gale, Nathan stayed indoors.

5. My dog likes digging old bones out of the yard.

6. He wanted to see the crystal cave before he left.

7. A sick friend of mine rallied after taking her medicine.

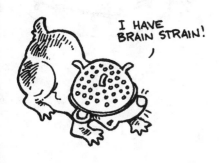

I HAVE BRAIN STRAIN!

Digger The Mole Dug A Great Big Hole

Digger is in trouble.

Help him find his way safely back to his burrow.

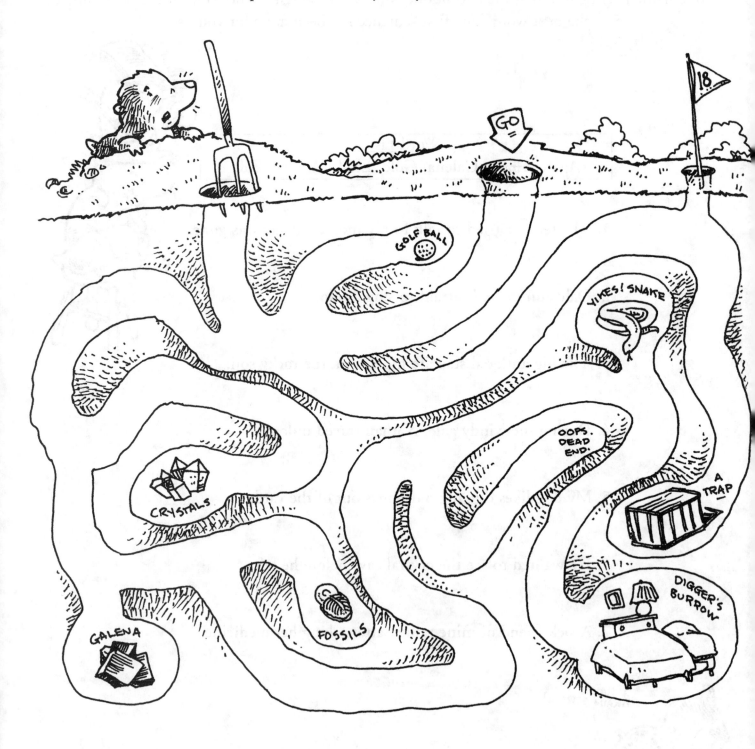

"WHICH IS MY FAVORITE GEMSTONE?"

Circle these gemstones in the puzzle:
BARITE, CALCITE, GALENA, HEMATITE, MARCASITE, PYRITE, SPHALERITE

They can be found down and across.

```
B   U   R   S   L   I   O   S   H   G
A   M   J   P   Y   R   I   T   E   K
R   X   F   H   V   I   A   C   M   I
I   U   S   A   T   O   I   A   A   L
T   G   A   L   E   N   A   L   T   X
E   M   H   E   C   K   I   C   I   A
I   M   A   R   C   A   S   I   T   E
J   H   M   I   W   R   T   T   E   I
F   W   N   T   Y   K   G   E   K   I
Y   R   O   E   L   S   D   A   C   K
```

Fill in the blanks with letters from one of the gemstones above to find Digger's favorite gemstone.

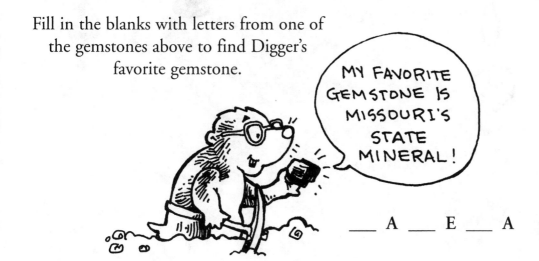

MY FAVORITE GEMSTONE IS MISSOURI'S STATE MINERAL!

__ __ A __ __ E __ __ A

Find the gem's shadow

Draw a line from the gem shape to its matching shadow.

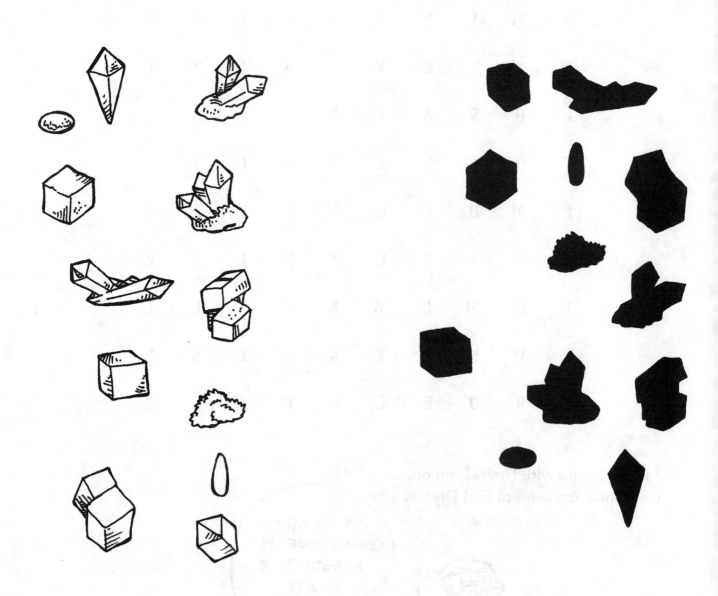

Who Were the First Miners?

Native Americans and their ancestors were Missouri's first miners.

Circle the things Native Americans might have made with the minerals they found.

A Magnet Mine in Missouri?

Design some refrigerator magnets for Digger.

His favorite things are
rocks, fossils, and friend Batty.

The ore that makes magnets is called magnetite.
Magnetite is mined at Pea Ridge Mine in Sullivan, Missouri.

Digger Discovers the Jabberwocky Rock

When lightning hits the sand, it can instantly make a Jabberwocky rock.

YIKES!

Cross out every third letter to discover the real name of Digger's Jabberwocky rock.
Then write the remaining letters in order on the blanks below.

__ __ __   __ __ __ __   __ __ __ __ __ __

__ __ __ __ __ __ __ __ __

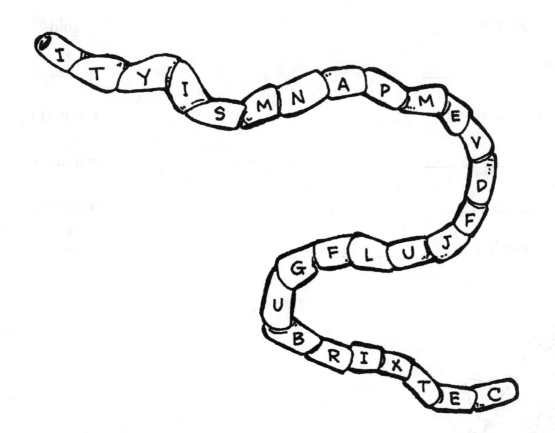

Scrambled words

Unscramble the words for Digger.

Word List

1. A A G N L E _____   galena

2. E I E O R T M T E _____   gold

3. R I S V E L _____   iron

4. E I E A T T N G M _____   iron pyrite

5. D O L G _____   magnetite

6. N I O R _____   meteorite

7. N I O R R E P T I Y _____ _____   silver

ANIMAL ROCKS

Near Graniteville, Missouri, there are huge rocks shaped like an animal.
One of the rocks is even called Dumbo.

Connect the dots below to learn what animal these rocks look like.

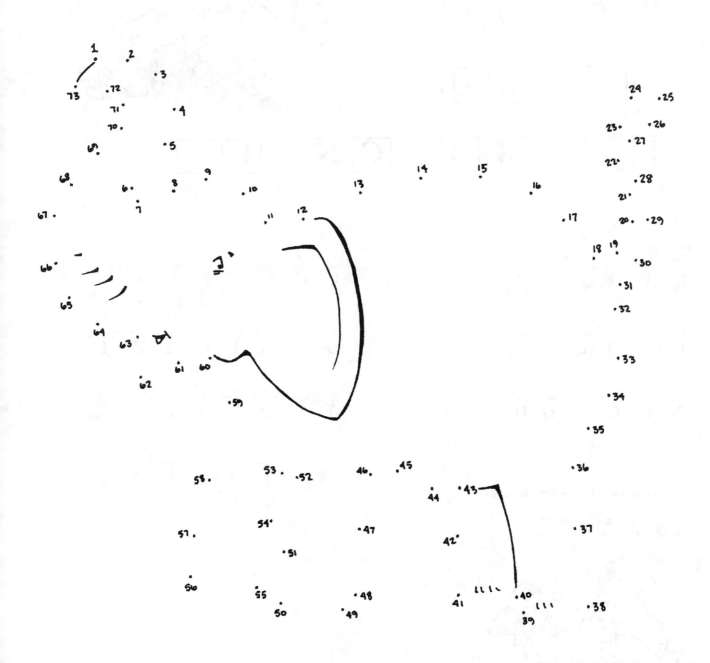

"We're Partners in Gemstones."

Discover the names of some Missouri gemstones.

Look for a letter under each line.
Find it in a square and write its letter partner on the line.

H	M		Q	R
Z	T		O	F
P	Y		A	U
I	E		X	B		G	N		C	L

Q U
‾‾ ‾‾ ‾‾ ‾‾ ‾‾ ‾‾
R A U Q Z T

‾‾ ‾‾ ‾‾ ‾‾ ‾‾ ‾‾
X U Q E Z I

‾‾ ‾‾ ‾‾ ‾‾ ‾‾
N U C I G U

‾‾ ‾‾ ‾‾ ‾‾ ‾‾ ‾‾
L U C L E Z I

‾‾ ‾‾ ‾‾ ‾‾ ‾‾ ‾‾ ‾‾
O C A F Q E Z I

‾‾ ‾‾ ‾‾ ‾‾ ‾‾
Y P Q E Z I

‾‾ ‾‾ ‾‾ ‾‾ ‾‾ ‾‾
M I H U Z E Z I

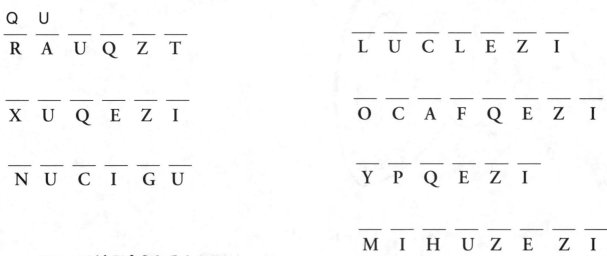

THIS ONE IS TOO BIG, BIG BIG!

YEAH. MY EYES WERE BIGGER THAN THIS HOLE!

TONGUE TWISTERS

Say these tongue twisters five times in a row as fast as you can.

1. Ruth rocks and rolls on real rocks in her rocker.

2. Silver slivers shine and shimmer.

3. Digger digs dirt down underground.

4. Batty B. Bat bites big bugs.

5. Many minerals make many mountains.

6. Round and round the river rolls the rocks.

Taum Sauk Mountain

Taum Sauk is Missouri's highest mountain. It stands 1,772 feet in height.
It is made from igneous (volcanic) rock.

Count by 2's to connect the mountain below.

"Where do they belong?"

Write each word in the word list in the most appropriate column.
Some of the words can be found in more than one place.

WORD LIST

bats, beetle, cave beetle, cave popcorn, chisel, chocolate bar, column,
field guide, gloves, grass, hammer, hand lens, moles, newspaper, rocks,
rock soda straws, seeds, stalactite, stalagmite, stone lily pads, worms

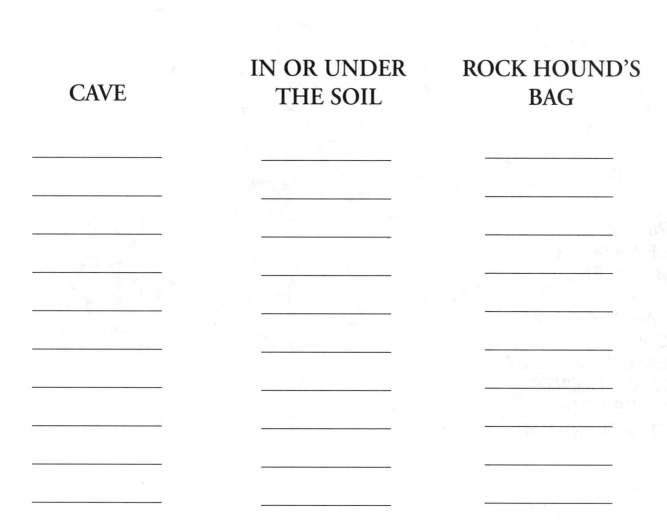

CAVE	IN OR UNDER THE SOIL	ROCK HOUND'S BAG
_____	_____	_____
_____	_____	_____
_____	_____	_____
_____	_____	_____
_____	_____	_____
_____	_____	_____
_____	_____	_____
_____	_____	_____
_____	_____	_____

ANSWER KEY

Page 2:

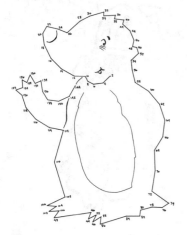

Page 3:

Page 5:
NEWSPAPER
HAND LENS
BAG
HAMMER
CHISEL
SAFETY GOGGLES
HEAVY GLOVES
GUIDE BOOK
CHOCOLATE BAR

Page 6:

Page 7:

Page 8:

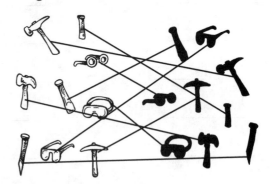

Page 9:

Page 11:
Sedimentary
Metamorphic
Igneous

Page 12:

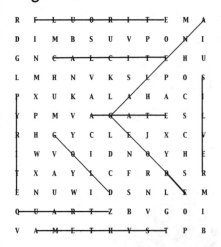

Page 13:

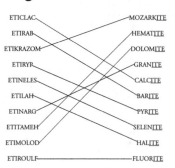

ETICLAC — MOZARK<u>ITE</u>
ETIRAB — HEMAT<u>ITE</u>
ETIKRAZOM — DOLOM<u>ITE</u>
ETIRYP — GRAN<u>ITE</u>
ETINELES — CALC<u>ITE</u>
ETILAH — BAR<u>ITE</u>
ETINARG — PYR<u>ITE</u>
ETITAMEH — SELEN<u>ITE</u>
ETIMOLOD — HAL<u>ITE</u>
ETIROULF — FLUOR<u>ITE</u>

Page 15:

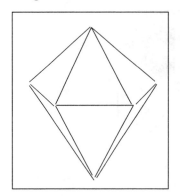

Page 16:

Page 17:
Hand lens
Heavy gloves
Hammer
Bag
Safety goggles
Chisel
Newspaper
Guide

Page 18:

Page 19:
Mastodon

Page 20:

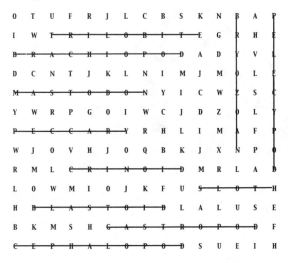

Page 21:
Blastoid
Crinoid
Gastropod
Digger

Page 22:

crinoid stem

plant fossil

blastoid

brachiopod

trilobite

gastropod

Page 23:
Agate — gate, ate, at
Quartz — quart, art
Magnetite — magnet, net, it
Flint — lint, in
Granite — ran, an, it, nite
Hornblende — horn, or, blend, lend, end
Crinoid — in, no
Anthracite — an, ant, it
Echinoidea — chin, in, no, idea
Pumice — mice, ice
Galena — Gale, ale
Graphite — Graph, rap, hit, it
Limestone — lime, limes, me, stone, one, on, ton, to, tone
Mozarkite — ozark, ark, kite, kit, it
Amethyst — me, met, thy
Elephant Rocks — an, ant, rock
Fool's Gold — fool, old
Gypsum — sum
Halite — lite, lit
Trilobite — lob, bite, bit, it
Olivine — vine, in

Page 24:

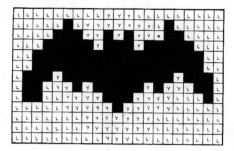

58

Page 25:

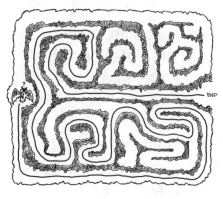

Page 26:
Ozark Big-Eared Bat
Gray Bat
Eastern Pipistrell Bat
Indiana Bat
Big Brown Bat

Page 27:

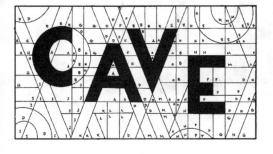

Page 28:

Page 29:
1. Stalactites
2. Stalagmites
3. Columns
4. Draperies
5. Cave pearls
6. Rimstone dams
7. Popcorn
8. Helictites
9. Soda straws
10. Lily pads

Page 30:

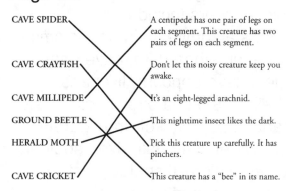

CAVE SPIDER — A centipede has one pair of legs on each segment. This creature has two pairs of legs on each segment.

CAVE CRAYFISH — Don't let this noisy creature keep you awake.

CAVE MILLIPEDE — It's an eight-legged arachnid.

GROUND BEETLE — This nighttime insect likes the dark.

HERALD MOTH — Pick this creature up carefully. It has pinchers.

CAVE CRICKET — This creature has a "bee" in its name.

Page 31:

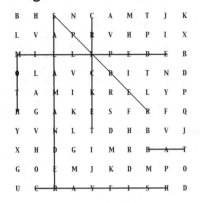

Page 32:

Answers will vary.
Possible answers include:
stalactite, stalagmite, column, dolomite, limestone, rimstone dam, cave pearls, draperies, cave popcorn, lily pads, onyx, helictites, soda straws, blind fish, salamander, bat, cricket, transparent crayfish, water, waterfall, river, spelunker (a cave explorer), speleologist (someone who studies caves).

Page 33:

Page 34:

Answers will vary.
Some words from stalactite include:
a, lit, lite, state, at, ate, late, cast, last, it, sit, tis, cat, talc, steal, site, stale, cleat, lest, let, set.

Some words from stalagmite include:
a, stag, lag, at, ate, late, last, it, sit, tis, steal, stale, lest, let, set, get.

Some words they have in common include: a, at, ate, late, last, it, sit, tis, steal, stale, lest, let, set.

Page 35:

Page 36:
1. Paleontologist
2. Geologist
3. Metallurgist
4. Speleologist
5. Seismologist
6. Archaeologist
7. Meteorologist

Page 37:

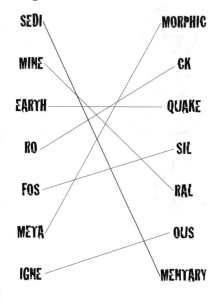

SEDI — RAL
MINE — OUS
EARTH — QUAKE
RO — CK
FOS — SIL
META — MORPHIC
IGNE — OUS

Page 38:
Answers will vary.
Some three-letter words include:
art, ear, the, eat, rat, sat, set, tea, sea, sue, hat.

Some four-letter words include:
heat, seek, here, hear, rake, sake, hate, rate, rest, seat, hurt.

Some five-letter words include:
quake, steer, queer, stake, sheet, heart, there, quest.

Page 40:
1. 4
2. 8
3. 7
4. 5
5. 7

Page 41:

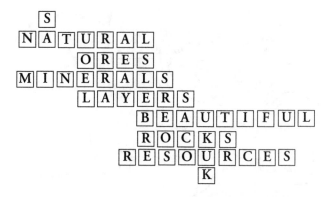

S
NATURAL
ORES
MINERALS
LAYERS
BEAUTIFUL
ROCKS
RESOURCES
K

Page 42:
Words that should be crossed out:
rose, violet, dandelion, tulip, centipede, millipede, beetles, tea, coffee, worm.

Word that remain: jewelry, paper, cement, batteries, foil, sheet rock, plumbing pipes, china dishes, money, soap, sunscreen, paint, salt, pans, bricks, trumpet, cans, medicine.

Page 43:

2. Dale admits he is afraid to sing a solo.

3. The big antlered stag ate moss from the rocky soil.

4. During the windy gale, Nathan stayed indoors.

5. My dog likes digging old bones out of the yard.

6. He wanted to see the crystal cave before he left.

7. A sick friend of mine rallied after taking her medicine.

Page 44:

Page 45:

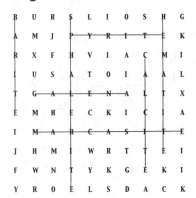

Galena

Page 46:

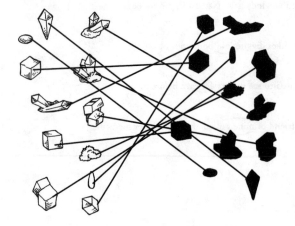

Page 47:

Page 49:
It is named fulgurite.

Page 50:
1. Galena
2. Meteorite
3. Silver
4. Magnetite
5. Gold
6. Iron
7. Iron pyrite

Page 51:

Page 52:

Q	U	A	R	T	Z
R	A	U	Q	Z	T

B	A	R	I	T	E
X	U	Q	E	Z	I

G	A	L	E	N	A
N	U	C	I	G	U

C	A	L	C	I	T	E
L	U	C	L	E	Z	I

F	L	O	U	R	I	T	E
O	C	A	F	Q	E	Z	I

P	Y	R	I	T	E
Y	P	Q	E	Z	I

H	E	M	A	T	I	T	E
M	I	H	U	Z	E	Z	I

Page 54:

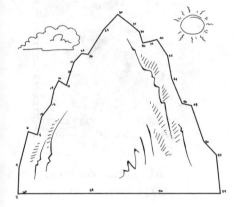

Page 55:

CAVE	IN OR UNDER THE SOIL	ROCK HOUND'S BAG
bats	beetle	chisel
cave beetle	grass	chocolate bar
cave popcorn	moles	field guide
column	rocks	gloves
rocks	seeds	hammer
rock soda straws	worms	hand lens
stalactite		newspaper
stalagmite		rocks
stone lily pads		

63

Take off with the *Alpha Flight Books* Series!

Here's a series of hardcover jacketed ABC books that will teach children the alphabet while also giving them interesting information about each letter's topic. The series is designed for the preschool and beginning reader, but its format and fun facts make it suitable for ages 4-8. Each letter of the alphabet will have a two-page spread consisting of:

• the letter in both upper and lower case • a three to four sentence explanation of each letter's topic
• a photograph • illustrations

"C" is for California
1892920271 • $17.95

"C" is for Canada
1892920301 • $17.95

"M" is for Missouri
1892920263 • $17.95

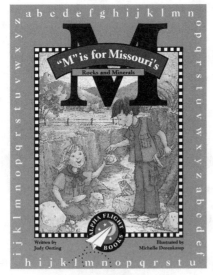

**"M" is for Missouri's
Rocks and Minerals**
1892920298 • $17.95

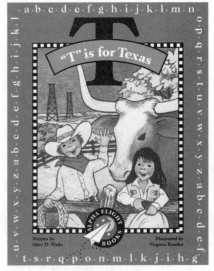

"T" is for Texas
189292028X • $17.95

GHB Publishers

**3906 Old Highway 94 South, Suite 300 / St. Charles, Missouri 63304
888-883-4427 / FAX: 636-441-7941 / www.ghbpublishers.com**